Aisha!

May this book provide insight,
encouragement, and be fruitful
in your life and in the lives of
those you share it with. God bless
you and may He keep you always!

Kennett Spurs

BETWEEN HOMES

RAISING CHILDREN IN SINGLE OR CO-PARENT HOMES

Copyright
Between Homes: Raising Children in Single or Co-Parent Homes
Kenneth Spresley

© 2018, Kenneth Spresley
Self-publishing
Contact@KennethActsOut.com

ISBN 978-1-64370-191-2

Printed in the United States of America

DISCLAIMER:

This book is designed to provide information and motivation to our readers. It is sold with the understanding that the publisher and author are not engaged to render any type of psychological, legal, or any other kind of professional advice. Neither the publisher nor the individual author shall be liable for any physical, psychological, emotional, financial, or commercial damages, including, but not limited to, special, incidental, consequential or other damages. Our views and rights are the same: You are responsible for your own choices, actions, and results.

BETWEEN HOMES

RAISING CHILDREN IN SINGLE OR CO-PARENT HOMES

KENNETH SPRESLEY

Dedicated

To my sons, Christian and Jacob,
always strive for greatness! Without you two there
would be no reason for me to write this book. I love
you both.

ACKNOWLEDGEMENTS

The inspiration to understand the need for this book came from challenges in my life that God allowed to manifest. Each challenge has refined me in my faith, leadership, exhortation, and discernment. So I want to acknowledge and give Him thanks first and foremost for molding me through these challenges of life, and I want to thank Him for introducing me to many angels along the way that have helped to steer me in the direction of completing the good works He predestined for me to accomplish.

One of the angels God sent was best-selling author, Payne Harrison. I recall our short Uber ride together as we found ourselves sharing our history, goals, and interests. God could have chosen any Uber driver that night, but he chose one that I would really feel inspired by and one who would help me realize the need between writing a book about business or one that speaks to a generation living with children in single or co-parent homes. Your feedback and recommendations were taken to heart, and they have been the direct push for what you see today. For that I want to thank you!

Another angel is my grandmother. Although you will never read these pages, I know you are in heaven smiling, because I came in this world and made a difference! I will have you in my heart for an eternity, and your lasting impression on me will be a legacy I hope to continue throughout the generations. And to be completely honest you were the catalyst in many ways as to why I am who I am and why I am here to tell the story.

I want to also thank my wife, Tanasha Friar-Spresley, for her support. She allowed me to dedicate many hours to the writing process throughout our courtship, and has been resourceful in her efforts in helping me transform this book into something that is clear and concise for readers at different levels.

Cheryl Polote-Williamson is another person who has dedicated her time, extended network, and tips to my development as an author. Her vigorous spirit and passion as a leader has been instrumental in my life. Not once did Cheryl say she was too busy to invest her mentorship into me— when she obviously could have.

I want to send a special thanks to my mother for all of her sacrifices as a single mother in my life. Her persistence through trials in her life are reason enough why I am here today. Thanks to my step-dad, Johnnie Wynn, for his desire to step up to the challenges of raising two kids that were not his biological offspring, and to my grandfather for being the father figure I needed when I had no fatherly examples around me to model after.

Thanks to my spiritual mother-in-Christ, Dr. Nancy C. Turner, for pouring encouragement, love, and her time into me! Also, there are many others, who have helped along the journey, those who have shared their struggles and accomplishments with raising children in co-parent or single parent environments, and those who have provided encouragement, insight, and tips for launching this book. Last, but not least, I want to thank you, the reader, for picking up this book, whether it was gifted, borrowed, or purchased. Your support means everything to me. May God bless and keep each of you!

TABLE OF CONTENTS

BETWEEN HOMES | YOU'RE NOT ALONE

"The LORD is the one who will go before you. He will be with you; he will not leave you or abandon you. Do not be afraid or discouraged."
Deuteronomy 31:8 (CSB)

July 31st, 2012, is a date that has been etched in my memory. On that day, who would have thought my life would have been shaken up so drastically that I would be here writing a book to share the story? I do not want to give you the wrong impression though. This is not a story about how hurt I felt when my ex-wife wanted a divorce, nor is it a 12-step program of how to get over your ex in 30 days. This story is about remembering we are all weak; however, we are made strong through Christ Jesus. And it focuses on our responsibilities as parents to our children, whom we forget become caught up in the middle of our fractured and failed relationships.

Six years ago if you had told me "this situation will make you stronger than ever before, and you will minister to others," I would have laughed. In those moments of darkness it is hard to see any light at the end of the tunnel. It becomes challenging enough just to do simple tasks around the house let alone believe that you will rise up from this "death" you are experiencing. However, you would have been correct, and like the old saying goes "hindsight is 20/20" and I have had my fair share of "20/20" experiences—this being one of them.

As I unpack the information and experiences in this book, I want you to know something that I needed to know when I became faced with the challenge of raising my son in a co-parent home—YOU'RE NOT ALONE! Also, recognizing that everyone does not have a co-parent environment and may be single parents raising kids my advice is still the same—YOU'RE NOT ALONE! I needed to hear that when I was beating myself up. I needed to hear that when I was asking myself, "What could I have done differently?" I needed to hear that when I was placing all the blame on me. I needed that sooner than I got it nearly three years ago. So, prayerfully you have just picked this book up in the season of your life when you need to hear the words—YOU'RE NOT ALONE! This book in no way is intended to rush you along to becoming the parent you need to be in a day or two. It is, however, intended to plant a seed that should flourish into a beautiful relationship between you and your child over time.

My story is very similar to a lot of stories I'm sure. A story that starts off happy. Then it ends with disappointment and regrets. A story where two people meet and experience love that was different from all of those past relationships, and maybe they even get married. Then, before they know it, they are sitting in the mirror asking, "What was I thinking?" Memories of what friends and love ones shared begin to echo in their minds. The gestures of how others felt toward the person once thought of as that "forever love" sticks out like a sore thumb. In some instances, those people reconcile their differences. In other instances, they will move on and possibly find new love. Some may never have to deal with their past significant other ever again. Yet in most cases, there is a child sitting in the center of the *battlefield of love* torn by the divide and often times overlooked. I want to pause for a second right here. I want you to really take that in. Close your eyes and envision that battlefield. Visualize how it starts in this beautiful place of nature with flowers in full bloom. Inhale around you and you will smell the hint of everlasting love and beautiful creation. In that beautiful place, imagine it changing gradually into a place of destruction. Picture the trees scorched, flowers withered, smoke, and the smell of sulfur, and in the middle of that is the beautiful creation made before it got to that point—your child.

That's where I want to call your focus. That's where it really matters right now. Yes, your emotional wellbeing matters too. However, we tend to spend so much more time on our needs and selfishly forget about the emotional needs of the child sitting on that battlefield. Some of us jump from failed relationship to failed relationship trying to fix our emotional needs yet the child in the middle is neglected or at the most malnourished in the required emotional stability.

In today's society, it's such a priority to find ways in making co-parent and single parent homes work. Shockingly enough, census and survey data has shown a rapid decline in two-parent first marriage homes where less than half of the kids in the United States live in two-parent homes. A Pew Research Center revealed that in the 1960s, 73% of kids in the United States, under the age of 18 years old, lived in a two-parent first marriage home. By the 1980s, that percentage declined to 61% and fell to 46% by 2013.

This is where the challenge comes in. With so many kids growing up in co-parent and single parent homes there is much to consider as we look at the difficulties the child could experience while meeting their psychosocial development stages. In 1963, theorist Erik Erikson addressed these development stages of life from infancy throughout adulthood. Through my study and understanding of his theory, I find the most interesting stages of Erikson's *Stages of Psychosocial Development* take place from the ages of infancy through adolescence. He does notate further challenges that young adults through late adulthood confront. However, for the purpose of this book, we want to stay in these early stages of development for a moment. Although we know there are unique challenges in the lives of many adults. In some cases, many were raised in single parent homes themselves, or in dysfunctional two parent households. Some, now adults, had parents that were disengaged in meeting their emotional, psychological (mental), social, and spiritual needs, during such critical and early moments of childhood development. I believe that if we, as parents, get the early stages right with our children, adulthood will be much easier for them to manage.

I studied Erikson's theory back in 2008 while stationed at a small Italian Air Force base tucked away in Northern Italy. During this time, I was also taking a psychology class online at the University of Maryland, and I was expecting my first child. So I'm sure you can imagine it was a pretty exciting time back then! I was extremely fascinated with anything that spoke about childhood development and the advancement of such development. This is around the time that Erikson stood out to me. He identified issues of *trust versus mistrust (during infancy to 1 year)*; *autonomy versus shame and doubt (1 to 2 year olds)*; *initiative versus guilt (3 to 5 year olds)*; *competence versus inferiority (6 year olds to puberty)*; and *identity versus role confusion (teen years into 20s)*.

Erikson's theory was likely influenced by his own life experiences. He was born the son of a Jewish mother and a Danish father, and was considered to be an outsider on both sides. Erikson was scorned as a Jew in school and mocked as a Gentile in the synagogues. I can only imagine how he felt when he heard Jesus Christ came for the Jews and the Gentiles. Just teasing!

19

Although his upbringing likely influenced his theory of psychosocial development, I don't believe Erikson was far off. Think about the lessons that we teach our children verbally versus non-verbally and directly versus indirectly. As parents, how we deal with trust often will reflect the way our children trust others. In today's world, many of us do not see a problem with children and their mistrust for people—especially with strangers. In a world corrupt with evil thoughts and intentions, who can blame them? I am an advocate for teaching trust boundaries. In many ways, that begins with having an open and trustworthy relationship with your child.

You may be thinking how an infant could possibly learn trust. While this might be hard to digest, babies are always learning through all available senses to discover and understand this new world they live in. When we soften our voices and smile, over time the baby begins to identify that action—to symbolize a pleasurable experience. When we elevate our voices, especially to a point that causes fear, the brain signals the experience to be frightful or unpleasant. Now compound that with spoken words, gestures, and vocal inflection and it all comes together as the brain begins to cluster the information. That is just how our brain works.

When my son turned six months, I was eager to teach him American Sign Language. Growing up, I learned American Sign Language, and had the unique honor of having a deaf friend. After researching the benefits in reducing the frustration of communicating between both the parents and the child, I was onboard! My son's mother and I would sit and watch 30-minute puppet videos while our son would quietly absorb the information. We would then sign those learned signs to our son around the house. By the time he was seven months old, our son was able to perform basic signs. This helped tremendously with communicating his needs and wants. Once he began to talk, we left some signs behind. All in all, that was a remarkable experience. It really proved to me how smart children are even when they are months out of the womb.

I'm sure you can see how mistrust can be taught to our children at such early moments of life. Our parents likely taught us to have a "reasonable amount" of mistrust growing up. And it seems as the newer generations continue to come along and adjust to the world, as parents, we add to that already long list of "reasonable amounts" of mistrust. Think back when you were a kid. Did your parents tell you, "Do not talk to strangers?" How well did that go when a stranger would approach you and your parent in the grocery store and proceed to ask you your name? My parents would respond, "Did you hear that nice lady ask your name? Tell her your name." Now as newer generational parents, we have the same advice for our children. Instead when the stranger approaches, we answer for them.

Thankfully, my childhood was not completely restricted from the human population. I had a very interesting childhood. There were many people, experiences, and the different environments that shaped my perceptions of the world. I was a kid that lived boldly. I walked at least two to three miles from my elementary school to my grandmother's home, which by the way is something I would never let my son do in a million years! Today, that has more to do with my mistrust for people and some of the careless behaviors I've witnessed such as texting with both hands while driving. Who does that, right?

My grandparents and my mother were not like that with me. I would go to neighbors' houses, walk miles up the street to grocery stores, and walk miles to my cousin's house. My fears likely developed over time, as my grandmother would call me to the TV during the evening news broadcast about child abductions. I often credit this to gaining an understanding that some people do not have the best intentions. Also, I remember reading the milk cartons of missing kids and the postcards that we would receive in the mail. It was always concerning for me, as a kid, but it did not stop me from living bold and free yet cautiously aware of my surroundings. My upbringing was unique and with it carried a certain amount of "street smarts," so I was always prepared in case things got sketchy.

As a parent, I teach differently based on the changing culture. In fact, I often shock people when they find out I have a unique whistle for my son. Not that I think my son is a dog. I created it with the intention of not having to call my son's name in public places. My thought was to protect his identity from a stranger with sinister intentions. I'm not sure if abductions still occur the same way they occurred 30 years ago, but at the very least they would not obtain my son's name from me. We also developed passwords to verify if what a stranger says truly came from me. It's a precaution. It's teaching trust with boundaries.

Our parents often taught us who to trust and who not to trust. These lessons can carry over into the relationships we have with our children later as adults. I commend my mother for reserving her comments about my biological father growing up, and for allowing me to form my own opinions. She did not restrict us from visiting him when we wanted—even if we wanted to visit him in jail. However, she carried some precautions that, as a kid, I perceived. For instance, she would only sit in the living room of my grandmother's house at the edge of the couch. She did not roam around, nor stand up unless we were about to leave. Her body language signaled how uncomfortable she was, so following suit my brother and I did the same thing. We sat on the couch at the edge of the cushions.

When we finally moved out of the area, I recall my mother telling my brother and I to never disclose to our dad or anyone on his side of the family where we lived. So, when they would ask we would lie. I cannot say I blame my mother for the precautions judged by my dad's track record, but that only taught us that lying was acceptable. That was done in other ways too. Don't get me started on Santa Claus, the tooth fairy, and the Easter bunny!

Recently, I had a conversation with my mother, who, like many of you reading this book, was a single parent. We laughed over the various teachings of our parents that carried over into our parenting as adults. I was telling her about how my son tries to sneak toys out of the house, and how I found myself saying something she used to say, "You can't fool me. I've been here a lot longer than you!" We found that to be funny and ironic considering we wanted to become better parents than our parents. That is, we wanted to remove ourselves as far as we could from the old clichés. Does this sound familiar?

As you can see, parents are highly influential in the lives of their children, and just when you think your child is not paying attention to your actions that seems to be the time when they are learning the most. Think about your life growing up. How did your parents influence some of the decisions you now make as an adult? Whether those decisions included your church denomination, political affiliations, or some of your parenting norms— including how you discipline your child. How many of those teachings do you still follow?

If you are being completely honest with yourself you will see that these modeled behaviors and ideas have had lingering effects on the psychosocial stages of your development. Often, if we do not deal with our trust issues early, they fracture future relationships as we mature, and they tend to build walls when we enter into new relationships.

I want to reiterate something. I am an advocate for trust with boundaries. However, do you have mistrust for men based on how your mother viewed men, or do you have a mistrust of women from how your father viewed women and/or other men? Maybe you think all men or women are the same because of their views. Maybe your own experiences, while in fractured relationships, fed more into that perception. Wherever it stemmed from, it is vitally important to be conscious of it and approach it with caution because you very well could be passing your fears of trust to your children.

Thankfully, God knew we would be faced with such challenges! His Word speaks to these challenges and how we can get it right as parents. His Word is the foundation where we find strength and perseverance needed to get us through conflicts and struggles we may encounter along the way. Each chapter of this book is accompanied with a Scripture at the end of the chapter, which, through my experience, has proven to be more valuable than gems or rubies. I have experienced some valleys that have revealed how amazing God is and how faithful He remains throughout the ages. If you put your faith in Him, through the journey of co-parenting or parenting as a single parent, there is no mountain that will stand in your way!

God's Word teaches us how to raise our children, how to treat each other, and how to treat ourselves. And in case you did not know, it teaches us how to co-parent. Don't believe me? Read Genesis 16 about the story of Abram (later changed to Abraham) and Hagar. Before you do, let me set the scene up for you.

Abram was married to Sarai (later changed to Sarah). Sarai could not have kids and yearned to have her own offspring. So, Sarai suggested that Abram "knock up" her servant, Hagar. Like Adam, Abram listened to his wife and said, "Cool! Sounds like a great idea to me!" This obviously comes out of the KSV: Kenneth's Simple Version. Side note, I'm not sure if they used the term surrogate back then but it sounds eerily like "Sarah get," because Sarah was going to get her baby one way or another.

Hagar got pregnant with Ishmael and Sarai began to look at Hagar as worthless and worthy of scorn, or in the KSV, "She wanted to throw some shade." So, Sarai went to complain to her husband. Not wanting to deal with it, Abram did what a lot of men would have done. He told his wife to deal with it herself. I imagine Abram saying, "I'm not in it. This was your idea. Do what you want to do with that," and he slowly backed away.

What we see here is a repetitious story of a father removing himself from his responsibilities as a parent. By doing so, Abram allowed Sarai to deal with Hagar harshly. This caused Hagar to flee far away with the baby. Talk about cold-blooded and scandalous!

That might be hitting close to home for many of you already, but stick around there is more. Hagar fled into the wilderness. While miles away from home, she had an encounter with the angel of the *LORD*.

For many mothers, they probably would have gotten as far away from that negative situation as possible, and would have thought they made the best decision. However, the angel of the LORD told Hagar the opposite. The angel told her to return and to submit to Sarai, or in the KSV, "Go play nice, Hagar." Clearly, God knew and understood the importance of Ishmael being raised by both parents. And why wouldn't He? After all, He did create us.

You may have fled with your child because of a negative situation, and now you are miles from home and just like Hagar . . . YOU'RE NOT ALONE.

"

The LORD is the one who will go before you. He will be with you; he will not leave you or abandon you. Do not be afraid or discouraged.

Deuteronomy 31:8 (CSB)

(Also, see Jesus' last words in Matthew 28:20b.)

"For where your treasure is, there your heart will be also."
Luke 12:34 (CSB)

As I mentioned before, this book will focus more on the child, Between Homes, but let's face it in order to effectively accomplish what is needed for your child we have to deal with the matters of YOUR heart. We have to deal with the fractured relationships, the heartbreak, the roller coaster of emotions, the doubt, the anger, the guilt, the isolation, and the resentment.

In the midst of my divorce, I found myself going from one damaged relationship to another. Gradually, I would heal in some areas to be wounded again in others—yet I had to deal with the matters of my heart to get to an emotionally stable place. Much of that required a bit of counseling among friends, family members, significant others (at that time), and professionals. All of a sudden, like a light bulb going off, I realized that the only relationship that had not failed was my relationship with Christ. He never left my side even when I felt I had left His side. He was still there with the same love He had in the beginning. He was still providing His undying Light when my light was dimming. He was there to reveal that I needed a deep relationship with Him. Not just some personal experience but an intimate relationship with Him. I needed to know Him more than I had ever known Him in the past. During those extremely challenging times I would turn to His Word in an attempt to know Him. By turning to His Word, I would share it with others, set it as reminders throughout my home, and I would commit Scriptures to memory.

I recall having one of these moments and sharing an inspiring word on social media. A co-worker at the time had expressed that he had noticed my faith as I was going through such a difficult time, yet relied on God's Word. He had shared with me that he and his wife were considering a divorce. However, after witnessing the pain it had caused me, and through my faith, he opted to work on his marriage. Another similar story followed, which is when I realized that the experience I was dealing with was actually salvaging marriages around me, and those were just the ones that were told to me. What an amazingly honorable feeling!

For me, however, I was focused on the healing process and truly examining my heart. One way of doing that was by looking at what my Creator had to say about the heart. Jumping out of the pages of the book of Jeremiah were these words: "The heart is more deceitful than anything else, and incurable – who can understand it" Jeremiah 17:9 (CSB)? I was still struggling in my heart with anger and resentment toward my ex-wife that I had to deal with daily. Like most matters of the heart, these emotions were similar to roller coaster rides. There were some days that were [illegible] others that seemed extreme[illegible] would start off good and one c[illegible] from my ex would send the day[illegible] times I'm sure she wondered wh[illegible] apologizing when we had not had an[illegible] but in my head an argument took place a[illegible] where the apologies would come from. That'[illegible] would ask for her forgiveness. You see when[illegible] think ill thoughts toward someone it is like w[illegible] carried out on those feelings. Jesus speaks to that directly in Mark 7:20-23 (CSB) when He says,

> *"What comes out of a person is what defiles him. For from within, out of people's hearts, come evil thoughts, sexual immoralities, thefts, murders, adulteries, greed, evil actions, deceit, self-indulgence, envy, slander, pride, and foolishness. All these evil things come from within and defile a person."*

Oftentimes, anger can cause us to sin in our thoughts and we can think up some horrible things toward one another, which God sees as us missing the mark (sin). Although, we may have never actually carried out on any of those actions, we are still held guilty of the charges. In Matthew 5:21-22, Jesus gives a sermon on the matters of the heart:

> *"You have heard that it was said to those of old, 'You shall not murder, and whoever murders will be in danger of the judgment.'*

MATTERS OF THE HEART

s angry with his
be in danger of
r says to his
danger of the
u fool!' shall be

very clear. It is
s is a natural
time to time.
to guard your
ggesting what

...church at Ephesus when he said, *"Be angry and do not sin. Don't let the sun go down on your anger, and don't give the devil an opportunity . . ."* Ephesians 4:26-27 (CSB).

When Paul said, *"Don't let the sun go down on your anger...."* he was talking about how long we dwell in that space. Paul was saying, do not stay angry long. When we stay angry about a certain circumstance for too long we give the devil an opportunity to entice us to sin in our anger. That's when we start to think up all of the ways we can get back at that other person. This is a very dangerous place to be in, especially as a believer and as a parent. We tend to use whatever we can to hurt and/or spite a person we have become angry with, and sometimes we even use the child in the middle as an instrument to inflict pain.

Therefore, as much as we can, we should deal with each other in love, truth, and understanding. When we are upset with the other parent, we should express that from a place of conscious thought and rationality. Prior to the conversation, we should organize our emotional distresses and determine their source, and we should address them openly with love, truth, and understanding. In other words, we should strive to be more like Jesus Christ. Jesus communicated His message in love and in truth, and He came from a place of understanding the hardships that people face. Yet His truth never waivered— no matter how much people wanted to give in to self-indulgence and the ways of the world.

When you communicate to your child's father or mother, do you communicate from a place of love or do you communicate from a place of hatred or hurt? Are you completely being open in all aspects of the truth or are you closing off truth to avoid conflict or personal shame? Are you coming from a place of understanding the other parent's point of view or are you more focused on them accepting only your point of view? These are questions we must ask ourselves before and after we communicate with the other parent. More importantly we have to ask, "How does this conversation directly affect the environment, mental, emotional, and spiritual state of the child or children in the middle?"

We are reminded through the Scriptures that we should love one another as brothers and sisters in Christ. As believers, we should even love non-believers, or as the Scripture calls them, our neighbors. Without love for one another we cannot truly say we love God. In 1 John 4:20, the Word instructs us that...

> *"If anyone says, 'I love God,' and yet hates his brother or sister, he is a liar. For the person who does not love his brother or sister whom he has seen cannot love God whom he has not seen" 1 John 4:20 (CSB).*

That really makes you think about the relationships that surround you, and not just solely the romantic ones. Think about that father or mother who was not around when you needed them the most. Think about that friend you feel did you wrong, and now you never want to forgive them. What about that really racist or hurtful person you encountered? These feelings often hold us back from really growing into who God has called us to be, and literally you are lying if you say you love Him, when you don't love them.

Getting yourself to a better you is key to being the parent you need to be for your child. This will take some time depending on where you are in your life, but one important thing to know is you should not rush this process.

MATTERS OF THE HEART

DEVELOP AN INTIMATE RELATIONSHIP WITH GOD

God wants to have an intimate relationship with you. He made this clear by sending Jesus to pay the ultimate price for your sins and mine so that we may have fellowship with Him. To know Him is to know love. True love. The type of love that is undying, unwavering, sacrificial, and genuine. In fact, God is Perfect Love (1 John 4:18) and He will drive out all fear the more you build on that intimate relationship with Him. Therefore, dedicate time to reading the Scriptures daily. As your appetite for God's Word begins to increase, understand the context of those passages. I have found that a Study Bible is a great way to do this! However, if you do not have access to a Study Bible there are tons of other resources. I have included some in the Resource Section of this book.

In conjunction with reading God's Word, you should always be in prayer. The Scripture instructs us in 1 Thessalonians 5:16-18 to, *"Rejoice always, pray constantly, give thanks in everything; for this is God's will for you in Christ Jesus."*

That is pretty self-explanatory! You may be asking, "How can I rejoice when I'm still hurting?" Granted God never said it would be easy, but look at those blessings in your life, which should give you reason to rejoice. Whether the blessing is you still having a roof over your head, food in your pantry, lights in your home, breath in your lungs, or your sight to see, there is reason to rejoice. If you cannot find the joy there, think about your child in the middle of that battlefield. Surely you can find reasons to rejoice in the Lord even if it is for what He has done for you—not to mention the things that He has forbade happening to you such as death.

The second requirement the Scripture gives us is to pray constantly. Don't just pray over your circumstances, but pray for the father or mother of your child. Pray that God changes your heart toward them—especially if you still feel anger, resentment, or even malice toward them. God is the Ultimate heart doctor and we can see that all throughout the Scriptures!

Let me add, that the power of prayer is remarkable. Two things happen when you pray over something or someone: (1) either your heart changes toward what you pray about or (2) that which you have prayed about changes! I am a witness to its power, and I want to encourage you to continue to pray. As a matter of fact, I want to pray for you and with you right now:

Heavenly Father, thank you for your blessings! Thank you for who you are in the midst of my life and the life of the reader. God you know their heart, you know their mind, and you know their spirit. Give them what they need to get through the challenges of life. Provide them with a strength that can only come from you. Grant them peace that can only come from the Prince of Peace Himself! Guide their path righteously in Christ's name. Forgive us of our sins we have committed knowingly and unknowingly against you. We give you all the praise, all the honor, and the glory. In the name of Jesus Christ of Nazareth we pray. Amen.

When I was challenged with my divorce, I admit, it was hard to pray for the woman who I felt had destroyed our little family nest by wanting a divorce. Yet it was necessary not only for me, but it was necessary for her and our son as well. Somehow I knew if I didn't pray for her circumstances and her life, it would make things challenging for our son, who we share joint custody. I felt that he would have to face challenges his little mind was incapable of fully understanding. These were all but enough reasons to pray for her and our son more than my selfish interests.

The Holy Scripture reminds us that the battle is not against flesh and blood, "but against principalities, against powers, against the rulers of the darkness of this world, against spiritual wickedness in high places" Ephesians 6:12 (KJV). The battle is unseen through the naked eye—yet it is all around us. Therefore, we need to be in the spirit of prayer constantly to invoke the One who sees the seen and the unseen and judges righteously!

We must also give thanks. This seems simple right? To simply thank God when we have been

2

blessed with so much. Yet oftentimes, I feel when we are challenged and in the darkness of this world we are quick to ask for what we need or want, and slower to thank Him for what He has already done.

I recall when I was in that dark place of life, battling through a divorce, having a difficult time finding things to be thankful for. I was struggling in my finances, wanting to give up on life, and feeling like the system was unfair and unjust by requiring me to pay child support, although, I had joint custody. It was challenging to see any light at the end of the tunnel. However, all around me was light and beauty. It took time for me to get to that point. I remember being in one particular dark place. I wanted to end my life, but God, knowing my heart, used my son to send a message through song. I remember talking with my brother, and out of nowhere I heard this beautiful song. Thinking it was coming from my son's TV, I walked to his room. To my surprise, I saw my three-year-old baby boy sitting in his bed singing to the top of his lungs, "All night... all day... angels watching over me my Lord!" It made me realize that if I were to end my life, I would be no better than my father, who chose cocaine and a life of crime over me. At that moment, I realized that I could not leave him behind. It gave me reason to praise the Lord more than ever and to keep pushing through the adversity and challenges of life.

As I continued to put one foot in front of the other, it was then when I started to notice the sky with its beautiful arrangement of colors that I thanked God for. I recalled rainbows in a cloud and it would bring me to thank God, while remembering His promise to never flood the world again. Then, I would give thanks for the fresh air around me, the water that sustains life, the trees that produce oxygen for me to breathe, until it got down to just being able to breathe. I became thankful for the intricate yet simple system that just seems to work by His grace and mercy. I began to see how much I needed Him more and more as the days turned into weeks, months, and years.

SURROUND YOURSELF WITH GODLY PEOPLE

Let's just keep it real. Many of us have trust issues. Many of us have a hard time trusting people with our deepest emotional pains and details into our private lives. We've been betrayed at some point in life, or we have found ourselves becoming disappointed after having our expectations shattered. However, this is where discernment is critical in who we align ourselves with and who we share our thoughts with. Paul said in 1 Corinthians 15:33: *"Bad company corrupts good character."* This should be applied in all aspects of our relationships with people. If you keep yourself in the company of people who gossip, lie, steal, and/or cheat, you are setting yourself up to be corrupted in your character, and it will compromise who you

41

are as a person. Therefore, seek friends and family members who strive to exhibit the fruit of the Spirit, which are love, joy, peace, forbearance, kindness, goodness, faithfulness, gentleness, and self-control.

Usually we can tell if a person exhibits these qualities by observing how they apply these characteristics with other people around them and in their life. We tend to observe these qualities in people, and we may commend them for having a good heart. Take notice of people like this in your life and begin to build a rapport with them. These people should offer sound and truthful advice— even when it is advice you do not want to hear. These types of individuals will tell you to forgive when you do not want to, and will give you advice from a biblical perspective and not from their dysfunction or troubled past.

Naturally we look to align with people who will jump to our side in the midst of conflict—yet these people are not always ideal candidates for giving sound and truthful advice. They care about you deeply, which is why they are willing to come to your defense and fight for you. However, they speak softer truths that really are geared toward building more walls than breaking them down. These group of people can be family members or close friends and like you they are dealing with their disappointments, pains, and emotional scars that could have come from previous relationships or from your relationship. If it is a parent, they are now losing or have lost a son-in-law or daughter-in-law they accepted and loved, shared private conversations with, or had certain feelings about since the beginning of the relationship. Now they see you going through a great deal of pain. It takes a highly rational, mind while in a highly emotional time to sort through the comments and advice offered by these types of supporters. We love them and they love us, but we must remain vigilant in what we receive in our heart. We have to understand where their comments and suggestions are coming from.

For me, I recognized that while going through my divorce I could only accept about 10% of the advice given to me by loved ones, because often they gave advice from their experiences in life. Through more questions about their lives and from what was already known I had to determine if the comparisons were apples for apples or if they were completely different. When really stacking up the experiences, I found that they were completely different in most cases, and when it came down to really gaining substance from those conversations, it was the 10% I could count on. It was the "Just pray about it," "God makes no mistakes," "Trust in God," and many other references that pointed to the Source of all things— God! These comments would have me seeking the Scriptures rather than running to the world with my concerns.

FORGIVENESS & FORGETFULNESS

"Forgive and forget." I'm sure you have heard this statement a time or two, and if not — keep living and you will. This is a default suggestion when people want you to get over your emotional struggles in life. They mean well because they want you to be well, but this phrase does not have a biblical foundation. However, there are many references advising us to forgive one another. In Matthew 6:14, Jesus says,

> "For if you forgive others their offenses, your heavenly Father will forgive you as well."

Therefore, unless you forgive others you cannot be forgiven for your offenses you have committed against God and this will hinder your fellowship with God. This is why forgiveness is so important. It does not mean you have to forget what happened, but it means you have to forgive the person that offended you.

I recall filming a testimony of one of the members at my church, who like many of us experienced some hardships as a kid growing up and later as an adult was still trying to put the pieces together. She mentioned something that really stood out from an exchange she had with the first lady of the church. The first lady had suggested the church member do one or the other . . . "Forgive **or** forget." With one word changed in the cliché, it has a more profound recommendation to either forgive or to forget about what happened in the past, which would lead to ultimately forgiveness in the end regardless, because it no longer becomes a crippling crutch residing in one's mind.

You see forgiveness is a conscious decision of our free will, and although by forgiving the offender it may never change their behavior, we know through the Holy Scriptures that God desires us to have a forgiving spirit. Jesus made it plain in Matthew 5:44, when He commanded believers to "love your enemies and pray for those who persecute you...." Paul echoes these words in Romans 12:14 when he says, "Bless those who persecute you; bless and do not curse."

It was challenging finding the courage to bless my ex-wife when I felt as if she was persecuting me and wanting me to lose everything— even if it meant losing the home where our son grew up. Since we've arrived on memory lane, I want to take time to share my story and testimony as we bring home the need for forgiveness.

In the early stage of our relationship (prior to marriage), I was a very young, self-sufficient, prideful, and arrogant airman in the United States Air Force. I had received a chance to live free from my mom and step-dad's rules and had begun to create my own rules in life. Many of these rules were influenced by the environment, social norms, and peers. As I began to learn more about who I was as a person. Many of you probably experienced this moment in college, or like me, you gained it during service in the military. However, I spoke very confidently and did not bite my tongue on what I had to say. I was very direct and honest, and spoke from my perspective. In many ways, I saw this as me expressing the hard truths. Prior to marriage, I really did not know what it consisted of and what was required. I based my understanding from my experiences growing up, which was dysfunctional at best, and what I had seen in popular movies. These were my examples to look to on how a marriage is supposed to work. They were definitely the wrong areas to seek marital guidance, but it was all I knew at 22 and 23 years old. When I reconnected with my soon-to-be wife, we both were coming out of dysfunctional relationships and neither of us had a sound biblical example of what a marriage should look like. In her childhood experiences, she grew up in a single parent home, and although I had a step-dad, it still felt like a single parent home with my biological father out of the family picture. So at best we were winging it on what a marriage should look like without a foundation.

I did not understand the role of a husband and the need to cultivate, nor did I have the understanding of sacrificial love. I spoke harshly in our disputes, directly to my thoughts, shutdown her rebuttals, and did not try to cultivate or grow her in the Word of God. As I matured, and as we overcame many of our challenges (I thought) I was becoming more of the husband I needed to be. However, at the end of the journey, she had already arrived at that place of being done with it all. She would later acknowledge that she had seen the significant changes in my attitude toward her, yet she still wanted a divorce. Initially, I declined her desire for a divorce, and twisted her arm to go through counseling. I was really trying not to ruffle feathers, but it seemed to drive her further away. We had gotten to a place where she had questioned her faith in God, and I had grown tired of being the only one trying to keep it together. When I had finally given my last attempt and efforts at saving the marriage, she confirmed that the divorce was what she wanted. After saving up the money to get a lawyer, for what promised to be a civil dispute, we ended up in a two-year divorce that tested the fabric of our friendship and faith at times.

However, through the challenges we faced, we have become a stronger parental front for our son because we have chosen to forgive one another. We know that sometimes we may not agree on things or on parenting methods, but we come from a place of love, truth, and understanding. We have also kept it central in our thoughts to put the focus on what's best for our son and his needs as a growing young man.

Since then, her family has grown. She has remarried to a really good guy, whom I'm blessed to have in this family partnership. He has really stepped up to the plate—willing to help in any capacity that he can. I cannot say that I know many men who would do some of the things he has done— aside from my step-dad.

"

For where your treasure is, there your heart will be also.

Luke 12:34 (CSB)

"I have given you an example to follow. Do as I have done to you."
John 13:15 (NLT)

I believe the most impactful people are those who are there in your life to inspire, cultivate, and encourage you to become better. Not because one day they hope to be pulled up in the ranks and they need all the allies they can get. I believe these people are impactful mostly because they love to see others happy and successful, and it is clear to see they live a hypocrisy-free life.

My grandmother, Louise Pettigrew-Bryant, was a remarkable woman. She was a woman who loved to serve people. She was a nurse, hotel owner, and she managed and operated her own in-home daycare where I grew up as a kid. I'm sure by now you can imagine where my entrepreneurial spirit comes from. She was a stern woman who did not allow people to take her kindness for weakness, yet she also loved hard. Sometimes that love came with a "switch" across the backside if you disobeyed her. Believe me . . . I know from experience. In today's era, she would be considered an authoritive leader. There were some decisions she allowed my brother and me to make on our own. Sometimes we were given a choice, and sometimes she would rule with the "iron fist." However, it was always a good balance. Neither leadership style would outweigh the other. In many ways it was easy to respect that and love her more

51

because of it. She was special to me if you cannot tell already. She taught me life lessons and allowed me to live boldly with a courageous heart. She inspired me to always strive for better, no matter what. She was there to cultivate my ideas and she would encourage me to keep out of trouble and to focus on whatever I was doing positive at the time. Not only was she impactful in my life, she was also impactful in the lives of the children who grew up in her home daycare.

For over 20 years, she raised children from infants to preschoolers. I recall in 2013, while I was going through my divorce, I went to check on her. Around this time she was riddled with Alzheimer's and early stages of dementia. As she sat on her porch, a group of young teenage boys came by on bicycles. They came to do the same thing I came to do. They came to see how she was doing and to see if she needed anything. We continued to talk more and one of the young boys said, "She used to take care of us when we were younger." In that moment, I thought "Wow! What an impact and legacy to leave behind." For these young boys something happened that inspired, cultivated, and encouraged them to serve others, and my bet is on her! She was that impactful.

As I grew up, I would help my grandmother in her daycare. I would teach the kids how to count, how to spell their names, how to read, and I would help prepare them for elementary. The most memorable kid was Larry, Jr. He was so eager to learn and he learned quickly. Before he started school, I taught him how to read, write, and spell his name. Of course, he learned his alphabets and how to count as well. I was so proud of him! I wish I could have seen him grow up to develop into the great person I am sure he would become. Unlike most of the kids at my grandmother's daycare, Larry had both parents in his life.

Some days his mother would drop him off and some evenings his dad would pick him up. Larry was a very lucky kid. When his parents would drop him off, I could not wait to tell them what he learned that day. I'm sure they fostered that environment or even replicated it at home for him, because he really had a passion for learning. Years later, as I went on to join the Air Force, I would always return home asking my grandmother about Larry, Jr. One year, I found out that Larry, Jr.'s mother passed away due to an illness. It was extremely heartbreaking to hear that, because I could not imagine what it would feel like to lose a mother at such an impressionable age. I thank God for the type of father Larry, Jr. had in his life.

As sad as it was for Larry, Jr. to lose his mother, it's even sadder with countless other kids just like Larry who grow up without fathers or mothers in their lives. In most cases, it's not because of death. They have either chosen to not be there, or have been restricted from being active participants.

My grandmother was one of nine children, and was the third oldest of her brothers and sisters. Her father, Roosevelt Pettigrew, and mother, Annie Pettigrew, were married for over 70+ years before my great grandfather passed away in 2005. They clearly had the secrets of a lasting marriage, and regretfully I did not have the foreknowledge or understanding of how significant that would be—especially among African Americans. To be fair, African American families have endured a great deal for nearly 400 years.

One of the most commonly used West African adages goes, "It takes a village to raise a child." This is derived from the unique family dynamic of kinship that extended vertically and horizontally among West Africans. Vertically, in the sense toward ancestors and children not yet born, and horizontally, which extended to the village. When the first Dutch ship with West African slaves arrived in America in 1619, their family life and purpose through community was destroyed. As slavery grew in America, slaves were not allowed to travel freely to find mates and the birthrate was low among African women. Some speculate the low birthrate contributed to the trauma of bondage. Others believe it was due to the longer nursing periods among Africans—which was considered a restoration period to promote sexual abstinence between childbirth. Some suggest the low birthrate had more to do with African mothers not wanting to bring their children into slavery. However, by the

18th century, African American women slaves born in Virginia began to have a higher birthrate compared to their African mothers, and bore children at younger ages.

This was not all that African American families had to overcome. African American families had little to no stability as slaves, unless they were on a plantation with a large slave population. However, that did not prevent a family from being separated and/or sold off to other slave owners. In addition to the lack of stability, the legal and religious institutions that supported family stability of White families did not recognize African American marriages. These institutions were often indifferent or even hostile toward the stability of African American families. The laws and the official church did not recognize slave marriages, simply because they viewed African Americans as property. However, George Washington did recognize marriages among the many slaves on his Mount Vernon farms. He records in a series of lists, in the summer prior to his death, that roughly two-thirds of the plantation's adult slaves were married.

Aside from the law not recognizing African American marriages and the separation of families, African Americans continued to endure opposition against the family through other ways, such as the crack cocaine epidemic in the 1980s that plagued predominately African American communities. In response to this, the US government sought to imprison many who were struggling with crack cocaine addictions. This epidemic impacted my life and family dynamic.

It was on a family trip to Los Angeles where the crack cocaine epidemic hit my family the hardest. During this trip, my dad took his first hit of the highly potent drug. As my mother recalled the experience, later in my young adult years, she told me that was when they experienced their first physical fight, which lasted on a long car ride from California to Texas. During that time, I was about three years old. Personally, I do not remember much of the fighting that took place on that trip. Nevertheless, I do remember other extremely traumatic incidents as a result of my dad being addicted to crack cocaine.

Today, as Americans face the opioid epidemic, we see laws have become less abrasive. When we look at who is impacted the most it is hard not to feel the system has been and will always be against the African American family. Don't get me wrong, great strides have been made for prison reform and drug addiction. However, much work is still needed in these areas.

Especially as we consider that of the 13% of African Americans living in the United States (US), they comprise to the highest number of jail and prison inmates. According to the US Department of Justice, in 2014, African Americans accounted for

35% of jail inmates and 37% of prison inmates. Coupled with the 13th Amendment, which was designed by nature to abolish slavery and involuntary servitude "except as punishment for a crime," the facts are hard to ignore that slavery found a loophole and continues to breakup the structural dynamic of the family.

With all of the adversity against the home, it is clear to see that the root causes creating single and co-parent homes are more complex than we could ever imagine or envision. However, our desire to create a healthy village for our children starts with us being the example they can model as they mature into adults.

"

I have given you an example to follow. Do as I have done to you.

John 13:15 (NLT)

"These words that I am giving you today are to be in your heart. Repeat them to your children. Talk about them when you sit in your house and when you walk along the road, when you lie down and when you get up."
Deuteronomy 6:6-7 (CSB)

As many great coaches will tell you, coaching starts before the game. Sometimes it starts before players become a part of a team. However, much of the foundation is laid during the countless practices. This is where they pour into athletes to gain the most athleticism from each player.

As a parent, you are the designated life coach for your child. You are the one who will likely inspire, cultivate, and encourage along the way. You are literally the example they will either want to follow or avoid following at all costs. Parenting is an action word; therefore, you cannot do it from the sidelines. It requires you to be actively involved. Not passively watching or attempting to instruct while standing by. It requires you to be there for as many of those first moments as possible. It requires you to give tough advice. It requires you to discipline. It requires you to pour on love and affection. It requires you to wipe the tears. It requires you to be a listening ear when your child expresses their challenges. It requires you to explain the things of this world. It requires so much more than what a passive parent can provide. Oh, just in case you thought I was talking about the other parent . . . I wasn't.

I was talking about you.

In life we get into a cycle. For many of us, we are chasing our tails during the day with the daily hustle of life, and when we get home we are in a vegetation state. This is our time to not have to think or focus on anything other than the programs we watch on TV. We do this, yet we tell our kids to finish their homework, finish their chores, do this, and do that when they have had an equally long day. As adults, we always think our problems are bigger, and some are, but we forget what it was like being a kid. They must deal with the social norms, the cliques, and the pressures to perform at 100% most of the time—if not all of the time.

Sometimes that will require us to turn off the TV, or whatever it is that keeps you from spending time with your child. This is critical, especially in a day where most of us spend a great majority of our waking hours away from our children. We give the task of raising our children to the daycare, school, and the after-school care providers. We drop our kids off at church for Vacation Bible Study or Wednesday night Bible study and come back when it's over. It has become our microwave-ready solution to parenting.

We have to find that extra strength to continue to build our children up and not leave this task to everyone else around us or to technology. When you depend on the world to raise your child, you do not know how much of what is being poured into their mind is wholesome. Proverbs 22:6 (ESV) instructs us to "train up a child in the way he should go; even when he is old, he will not depart from it."

Ask yourself:
How is social media training up your child?
How is the school training up your child?
How is that daycare training up your child?

As much as you want to answer those questions with something logical and wholesome, the truth is you cannot—simply because you are limited in your knowledge of what happens every second of the day. It is impossible for you to know what has been said or done to your child while in the care of others. Therefore, you have to train them personally. You have to talk to them about the challenges of life. You have to be the one to talk to them about bullying from cyber-bullying to physical bullying. You have to be the one who coaches them through their relationship challenges, and you cannot successfully accomplish that unplugged from your responsibilities as a parent.

I know what you are probably asking. How can I do all of that as a single parent? If you are a co-parent you might be asking the same question. I realize it is challenging, but as the old saying goes, "anything worth doing, is worth doing right," and raising your child is worth doing right.

However, that is not enough to motivate you alone. You have to recognize where your strength comes from. The apostle Paul was one who knew where his strength came from. Within the Bible we do not see much about Paul referring to a family or children of his own. However, we can tell that Paul saw the members of the early churches as babes in Christ. For Paul, it was his mission to nurture new believers with the Word of God and to bring them to an understanding of who they were called to be, and why they were called to continue to grow in their faith. Paul was definitely an encourager. We can see that in his writings in Philippians 4:13 as Paul declares the foundation of his strength. Paul wrote...

"I can do all things through him who strengthens me."

Paul was not talking about Peter or Apollos. He was talking about Jesus Christ being his strength. Don't believe me? Let's see what he wrote in his second letter to the church in Corinth:

"Therefore, so that I would not exalt myself, a thorn in the flesh was given to me, a messenger of Satan to torment me so that I would not exalt myself. Concerning this, I pleaded with the Lord three times that it would leave me. But he said to me, 'My grace is sufficient for you, **for my power is**

perfected in weakness' [author's emphasis]"
2 Corinthians 12:7-9 (CSB).

Theologians have struggled to understand what the "thorn" was which Paul referred to and have suggested that it was possibly his troubled past. Be that as it may, I am not a biblical theologian, so I will not attempt to understand Paul's thorn. I will say this, however: Your "thorn" as a single parent or co-parent allows the power of Christ to be exalted. Soon people will notice the efforts you put into raising your child while having a career and keeping your sanity! And believe me, they will ask you how you did it short of the grace of God.

I know this from experience. If I received a nickel for every time a person told me, "you are doing a great job as a father," I would be a very rich dad! None of that is by coincidence. No matter how much life weighs down on me I do not forget to enjoy life and delight in the simple things with my son. Bills will come and go. New problems will arise. Yet at the end of the road, I stand there with my arms wide open telling my son that I love and value him, and not just in word but in action. John, the disciple Jesus loved, said,

> "Little children, let us not love in word or speech, but in action and in truth" 1 John 3:18 (CSB).

You see . . . I made up in my mind and refused to become a passive parent. I chose to spend time with my son, meaning I did not send him away somewhere else every weekend like some type of inconvenience. He is worth more than that to me.

I would devote most of my time and energy to him while he was with me. This often meant that we would go do something together. Sometimes it was going to the park and flying kites. Sometimes it was an evening dinner at a restaurant. Sometimes it was putting Legos together at LEGOLAND. Sometimes it was going fishing. And sometimes it was just spending time at home playing video games, reading a book, or just talking. Whatever we did was our time. At times this meant that I would not go hang with friends, because that time with my son was/is the most valuable time we have together.

We still do stuff like this, because those are the moments you want your children to remember most. I believe time is the most valuable commodity we have, and when we use it as a parent to invest in our children it is wisely spent and creates a lasting and more enjoyable memory. Not the nagging mother who always told them to finish cleaning their rooms up or the provoking father who always pushed them to be a "real man" (as if cutting the grass made you more of a man).

These were the moments I recalled from my childhood. Which moments you ask? Both. I remember taking time out to go to the parks to ride bikes and spend time as a family. I remember the family game nights on Sundays, when my uncles and aunts would come over to play UNO, Chicken Foot, and Speed (card game), and I remember Monday movie nights.

However, I also remember the constant complaining about not being able to wash the dishes correctly or leaving a cup out from being washed. I remember the constant pull to cut the grass or work on the car. These were fine if maybe they occurred less frequently than simply spending time together as a family. There seemed to be an imbalance and it left me with more memories that were unpleasant as a kid than enjoyable ones. In fact, my step-dad and I bumped heads quite a bit as I grew into my teen years, mostly as a result of the constant push to perfection and harsh chastening. However, I also went through my struggle in finding my identity during those years, so I cannot place all of the blame on him. There are many valuable lessons he taught me growing up, especially lessons on how to be a loving step-dad if I ever married a woman with children. He would say, "If you ever marry a woman with kids, those are your kids too . . ." and he would say, "When people ask me how many kids I have I say 'I have four' and I don't have step kids...." In a time, where many relationships involved single parents and their children, this was knowledge that was wisely stored up for a time such as this one.

As I'm sure you can understand, spending time with your child is important, and I believe that you are **strong** enough to do it! And the reason you are strong enough is because you know where your strength comes from. And believe me, I'm not just saying this so you can share my book, I'm saying it because if you weren't strong enough, you would not be here right now reading this book. You would not be still standing and holding down all of your responsibilities you have as a parent!

YOU HAVE A PURPOSE AS A PARENT

My biological father was called into ministry at an early age. In a letter he wrote from prison, he shared with me his past and how he began preaching as a teenager. His father was also a minister who passed when he was still young. I'm sure this had a significant impact on his life. However, as he expressed to me in other letters, he did not turn from ministering until after divorcing his ex-wife (before my mother). This sent him on a spiral into a dark place, which over time caused grief and pain for many others in his path. Alcoholism would lead to drugs—crack cocaine being the strongest one to shake. The drugs led him to acting outwardly in his anger and aggression, which resulted in him murdering people, assaulting others with a deadly weapon, and abuse to those around him—some of whom were loved ones.

However, through it all, I am grateful to God that I did not have to grow up fully in that dysfunction . . . as much as I wanted my dad to be there. On the other hand, I would be in denial if I said his absence did not have an impact on my life. As I mentioned, when I entered into my teenage years I struggled with my identity. I had only one piece of the puzzle, which was my mother and memories of abuse, anger, and violence from my dad. In many ways, I hung to the negative attributes I recalled from my dad—the stories of gang life, selling drugs, and misogyny. I glorified it as a young teenager to my early 20s. I'm sure listening to gangster rap did not help it either. I would find myself jumping into that life all in an attempt to find my identity.

As time passed, and definitely after some military boot camp, my identity began to change tremendously. It had become so different that when my mother would tell me of things I did that reminded her of my dad, I would verbally claim to be nothing like him and would make conscious efforts to not follow his steps—even as it pertained to going into ministry.

In the Air Force, I wrote my dad while he was in prison. I wanted to understand the mind of this man who left many trembling in fear. I had no fear of him since I did not know him; therefore, I openly expressed myself through the letters. I resented him for choosing drugs over his children. More directly, I resented him for choosing drugs over me. I later learned a lot about him from hundreds of letters and prison visits. I learned about his character, upbringing, his flaws, insight, and abilities. Then, I would cross-reference his stories with those who knew him most—his siblings and his mother. In some cases, his stories would align and in others there would be a different variation to what actually occurred. Not that it was less heinous, but that it was more graphic than presented. He is still currently incarcerated and has been in prison now for almost 19 years after his last offense. I'm sure he has had plenty of time to think through some of the choices he has made in life. Even after all we have been through as a broken family, I still love him as my father—which took time as I grew up. It took time to learn how to forgive him at first, and then it took time to learn how to love him. We still talk from time-to-time through letters, and he has provided some encouraging wisdom in small doses throughout challenges in my life. And to be completely honest, I continue to learn about the deeply seeded history of my father's past and his father's past.

I was sitting with my childhood pastor and spiritual mentor over breakfast one morning, when he uncovered more "family curses" I had not been aware of until then. Although my spiritual mentor never knew my father, they both had the same spiritual father in ministry, Pastor C.B.T. Smith, who was also good friends with my grandfather.

Pastor Smith would recall the past and would talk about alcoholism being something my grandfather struggled with even as a pastor. After hearing this piece of information, it brought on the discussion of the role of the father and how the father provides a sense of identity for his children, and vice versa for a mother and her children. As we talked about that, it reminded me of a story that was shared during pre-marital counseling, before my son's mother and I were married.

The story went:

There was a wife who was preparing dinner for a family function. The husband stumbled upon the wife preparing the ham for the gathering. He noticed that she would cut large amounts of meat from the sides of the ham, making it into a small rectangular cube, while she placed it into a large pan. The husband, shocked to what he was observing, asked,

"Why did you shave off all of that ham and discard it."

The wife responded,
"That's the way my mother always did it."

The husband now actively seeking an answer went to his wife's mother and asked the same question. To no avail, his mother-in-law had the same response:

"That's how my mother always did it."

Almost feeling defeated and perplexed he asked his wife's grandmother. The grandmother, taking her time to explain, responded:

"When I would prepare meals for the family we were poor and had one small pan to cook out of, so I had to cut the sides of the ham in order for it to fit in the small pan."

Do you find yourself doing things because "that's the way your parents always did things?"

Yeah! I'm guilty of that too.

How do we become the example that is required of us? We first have to understand that we have a purpose as parents. Believe it or not, fathers and mothers have a unique purpose in the lives of their children.

When my ex-wife and I sat down to plan out how our child custody arrangement would work, we actually agreed on one very important idea: how important each of us would be in the life of our son. I knew, just as she knew, our son needed both his mother and his father. Each parent has a unique purpose, which is clearly described in the Holy Scriptures.

For a mother, she is given the important role of loving and nurturing her child and understanding that a child is a gift from God. Psalm 127:3 (ESV) proclaims,

> "Behold, children are a heritage from the LORD, the fruit of the womb a reward."

In the New Testament, the word *philoteknos* is used in reference to mothers loving their children with a special kind of "mother love." The word is thought of as meaning caring, nurturing, affectionately embracing, meeting the needs of the child, and embracing each child as a unique gift from God.

Mothers play a continuous role in the lives of their children no matter how old the child becomes. If you thought you would be done once they turned 18 years old, you are sadly mistaken. Motherhood does not end there! Fortunately, the role of motherhood changes over time; however, love, care, nurture, and encouragement for your children should never end. Paul writes Titus saying,

> " . . . teach the young women to love their husbands **and children** [author's emphasis]" Titus 2:4 (ESV).

When mothers are taught to love their children, there is no greater force on the planet than that kind of love. Part of the problem today is that we do not teach our young women how to love. Therefore, without those examples we bring over our limited understanding of love. Allow me to teach you how to love.

Love is patient and kind.
Love does not envy or boast.
It is not arrogant or rude.
It does not insist on its own way.
It is not irritable or resentful.
It does not rejoice at wrongdoing.

Love rejoices in truth.
Love bears all things, believes all things,
hopes all things, endures all things.
And love never ends.

Some of you reading that, probably thought that would make a great bumper sticker or poem, and although I agree, this was paraphrased directly from 1 Corinthians 13:4-8, and in case you did not get the humor, Paul actually wrote it . . . not me. Paul had a point though and he laid out the lessons of love.

I've heard ordained ministers recite these words countless times during wedding ceremonies, and ministers alike have read these characteristics of love from the pulpit. Usually, they equate all of that to mean the characteristics of God, which is correct. It is also teaching husbands, wives, mothers, and fathers how to love properly, and how to love like God.

In addition, Paul has a few words for fathers in the book of Ephesians:

> "Fathers, do not exasperate your children; instead, bring them up in the training and instruction of the Lord" Ephesians 6:4 (ESV).

In the KSV, "All you dads out there, don't make your kids angry by always responding with the 'switch.' Instead teach them why and how to do better through the Word of God."

As a father I know this can be difficult, because we want our children to have a better life than us. We want them to achieve more and, most importantly, not make the same mistakes we made growing up. We want this so bad for them usually to the point of exasperating them to meet these milestones. In my opinion, this drive to become better than us is rooted in fear rather than love. However, Paul instructs fathers to not foster negativity in their children through sternness, cruel demands, severity, needless restrictions, injustice, partiality, or through an unreasonable exercise of authority. Instead, Paul tells the fathers to educate their children by instruction and admonition of the Lord. We come to understand the word *admonition* carries the idea of constructive criticism to faults and teaching responsibilities. When applied properly, the child is taught to have reverence for God and respect for parental authority. They also gain knowledge of how to live as a Christian, and they gain habits of self-control.

In the theatrical film, *Fences*, Denzel Washington plays the character Troy Maxson. Troy is a hard working father and husband and in his eyes does the best he can to provide for his family. During one of the scenes, Troy tells a light, cheerful story (not really that cheerful) about growing up, revealing a difficult past to his oldest son, Lyons (Russell Hornsby) and friend, Jim Bono (Stephen Henderson). He told them that he was homeless at 14 years old. You can hear the pain of growing up in the house with his father. Troy defines the character of his father, which in many ways you see in Troy throughout the film. You begin to recognize what some would refer to as "tough love," rather than a sound biblical definition of love. Neither do you see Troy raising his children through the instruction of God's Word, nor remotely resembling what that would look like. Instead, he constantly provokes anger in his children and provokes them to fight him back physically or through arguments. There is a moment in the film that really struck a cord. Toward the end of the film, Troy's son, Cory (Jovan Adepo), looks at the recruitment poster for the US Marine Corp. Afterwards, he arrives home to a drunken father sitting on the stairs at the entry of the home. Cory expresses his need to get by Troy to enter the house, and thinking he would go around his dad, Cory is confronted by Troy. Troy stands and gets in Cory's face. Prior to this moment, Cory had lost respect for his father, since he betrayed his mother through infidelity. Due to the anger he has for his father, he feels Troy is not due the respect of being the head of the house, nor is he warranted an "excuse me."

This spoke directly to my life around the time I was about 18 years old. Although I cannot recall what triggered the argument between my step-dad and me, I remember saying that he did not love me, and it was the streets that loved me more. Before I knew it, he had pushed me into the wall of the bathroom causing the towel rack to cave into the dry wall. After that day, I moved out of my mother and step-dad's house. I stayed with my friend, Sirvel, a couple of nights, and to this day I don't think his mother ever knew. Eventually, I would stay with my grandmother and girlfriend at the time. Later, I headed down to the recruiters to join the Marines. After calling my mother to tell her of my plans to join the US Marines, she pleaded that I consider the Air Force. I am thankful I had sense enough to listen to her in that moment! No offense to my Marine brothers and sisters, but the Air Force is clearly the better branch and I mean that in love and in truth.

However, think about how much better it would have been if Troy had used God's Word to instruct his sons rather than use his frustrations and his anger to provoke them. I'm sure you've heard the saying: "it is better to attract more bees with honey." Well, God's Word is sweeter than honey (Psalm 119:103).

Two years ago, God sent angels to remind me of this while in counseling. My son had used some language at school that shook my core. It was impulsive, at the least, to hear such things come from your innocent little angel. He had expressed to a little girl that he wished she were naked, so he could kiss her. The school, of course, notified his mother and me, and they contacted the little girl's parents as well. As I'm sure you can imagine, her parents were not happy campers. I imagine they were probably a tidbit more upset than me in that moment, particularly because their little angel had been tainted with foul language.

Immediately, I knew I had to do something, and it had to be performed in a way that showed how disappointed I was—yet I did not want him to hate girls because of it. Also, I needed to understand where it came from. The next morning, I explained to him there would be serious consequences if that happened again. I threatened to take away all of the things that I knew brought him joy and yes, even to the point of corporal punishment.

After that conversation, I thought we had an understanding.

Nope.

Apparently we did not have a clear understanding of expectations. While at after-school care, he told a friend he wished his teacher's daughter, who he met at school, was naked so he could lay with her. At this point I was furious! I started thinking, "we JUST had a conversation," "I threatened to take everything from him," "I even threatened the belt," "what the heck is going on," and "where is this coming from all of a sudden?" I knew it did not come from our home, because I had taken a great deal of precautions to lock every TV with parental locks, and I knew it was not language that I used.

Fortunately, for him, he was with his mother that night and I had a counseling session that would later save him. Prior to my counseling session, my son's mother and I discussed the concerns we had with his behavior and had outlined his punishment as a direct result. However, after sharing what took place that week with the group at my counseling, session, there were a couple of ladies who reminded me that my frustration and anger would only lead him to hiding where those thoughts derived from.

After my counseling session, I contacted my son's mother and shared the insight, which ultimately meant the discipline approach would be slightly changed. We needed to understand where the thoughts were coming from. Of course, we had our suspicions that it could have been from the older kids at the after-school care, but we were not 100% certain. Initially, we were asking the wrong questions. We were asking the "who talks like this around you" and not the "what or where did you see this?"

After a very sincere conversation with our son, I discovered that one night, while at his other house, a late-night pornography show came on TV after a show he was watching. His mom and step-dad were asleep, so they were unaware that he was being exposed to that type of programming. We talked about how it was inappropriate for him to watch those types of shows, and I spoke to him about the responsibility to inform an adult if anything like that ever came up on the TV again and to change the channel.

Then I explained why from a biblical standpoint by going back to Adam and Eve. Believe it or not, even at 7 years old, my son knew more about the Bible than some adults, so it was not difficult to explain Adam and Eve's first sin, nor how God views lust. I'm giving you guys the adult version to the conversation, but as parents, especially as fathers, we have to teach our children God's instructions.

And I can say, since that conversation with my son, we have not had that problem again.

"

These words that I am giving you today are to be in your heart. Repeat them to your children. Talk about them when you sit in your house and when you walk along the road, when you lie down and when you get up.

Deuteronomy 6:6-7 (CSB)

"Death and life are in the power of the tongue, And those who love it will eat its fruit."
Proverbs 18:21 (NKJV)

"I was not ready to hear my son say he has two dads, but I think I handled it well with my response."

That was a statement I made on social media. As my son's biological father, it was a blow to my pride, initially. After I gathered my thoughts to what he was really conveying in those words, it was easier to respond. He was not telling me that my place in his life had been replaced, which is where my feelings wanted me to go. It was his way of saying, "I have two positive men in my life who equally love me and show it unconditionally." Obviously, he was aware of who I was as his father. It was clear that my position as his dad was secure; however, he now had a step-dad who loved him and expressed his love through providing for him and showing love toward him and his mother. So, when my son made the comment, I responded by letting him know that I love him and his step-dad loves him too. He needed to see there was no animosity toward his step-dad and that I supported a loving and nurturing environment for him.

Sometimes, in the heat of the moment, we can say or express things as parents that we wish we could take back. Mostly because our emotions did not allow us to convey how we intended for it to come out. We spend days or sometimes years wishing we could take back those words. There are also times where we openly express our thoughts to friends on the phone or in-person, and for a brief moment we forget we have our child around us, or we think they are distracted enough to not care about what is being said. This usually gets us in trouble, because the message either gets back to the other parent or the child begins to feel indifferent about the other parent.

When I was young, my grandfather became the father figure that I never had. I went everywhere with him. He took me on my first bus ride into Downtown Dallas, and I remembered we just walked around looking at the skyscrapers above. Anywhere he went I wanted to go with him. If he had a problem with something, which was not often, I had a problem with it too. I remember my grandmother had a guy friend who had a dry cleaning business out of his house. One day my grandfather and grandmother went by to drop off clothes. While sitting in the car with my grandfather, my grandfather said, "I don't like him." That must have set a fire in my pants, because I hopped out of that backseat so fast and ran up to the man and said, "MY PAWPAW DON'T LIKE YOU!"

Our children pick sides, believe it or not, and what hurts that parent hurts them as well. Therefore, we have to guard our emotions so that our children do not feel the need to pick sides. When things get fired up between you and the other parent, you have to learn to bite your tongue and let things cool down. That is a part of maturing through parenting.

The Scripture says, in 1 Corinthians 13:11 (CSB):

"When I was a child, I spoke like a child, I thought like a child, I reasoned like a child. When I became a man, I put aside childish things."

It is time to start reasoning like an adult now. The tit-for-tat has to stop. The jealousy for the success of one parent has to stop. The talking down of the other parent has to stop. We have to put aside all of the childish behavior and be the role model that God has called us to be as men, especially, and as women!

Recently, I watched an interview with the comedian Marlon Wayans on the Breakfast Club and found his interview to be enlightening and a great model to have for parenting your children. In the interview, Marlon talks about his NBC sitcom, *Marlon*. In the show, Marlon plays himself and projects for millions of viewers to watch dramatized and comedic scenes from events that have taken place in his life with the mother of his children, played by Essence Atkins, his son, played by my little cousin, Amir O'Neil, and their daughter, played by Notlim Taylor. If you have not seen the TV series yet you should definitely check it out on Netflix when you get a chance. The show depicts more of a lifestyle we should have with our kids who are innocent bystanders between homes.

During the interview, Marlon was asked, "Do you think people give up too fast on relationships now?" Marlon responded with some advice that should be echoed here again:

> "When there is children involved, you got to find a way to make it work. Because I do feel children need their mommy and daddy. A lot of . . . I think what's going on with society period is the fact that we ain't taking care of ours as men . . . WE HAVE TO DO BETTER. As women, WE HAVE TO DO BETTER. As Black people, WE HAVE TO DO BETTER."

Marlon went on to add how he explains conflict and how it is important to keep your word. He explained that after an argument with the mother of his children, he would let things cool down. However, before leaving their home he would explain to his children that disagreements happen from time-to-time, but it should not worry them because come the next day he would return to see them and that he loves them. Following that discussion Marlon says that he then would show up the next—staying true to his word.

What you say matters to your child. If you say you will come see them, fly them across the world to be with them, take them to school, pick them up, et cetera, they are depending on you to do that. Each time you do not follow through on what you say . . . you crush them and create a wider gap for mistrust to seep in.

In 2016, I took a trip to Los Angeles. It had been quite a while since I was last there in 1986, so we had some catching up to do. Prior to going, I explained to my son that his mother would take him to school during the time I was in Los Angeles. I've always given him a heads-up on how his weeks would go especially if they were outside of the normal routine, so this was a natural conversation. When I told him he asked if I would take him one day. I knew that was something I wanted to do, and I told him that I would definitely take him— even though I did not know when I would revisit. A few months passed and my cousin asked me to come down for the weekend to help with recording a song I had written and produced for her sons, Amir and Amari O'Neil, called "No Bully Zone."

There was a great deal of urgency with completing the song, because the twins were granted the opportunity to perform it in front of a crowd at a private annual celebrity charity event hosted by Stevie Wonder and his son, Kailand Morris, where proceeds went to the "All It Takes" charity.

Upon returning to Texas, I was excited about meeting Stevie Wonder, Anthony Anderson, Guapelle, Quinton Aaron, and many other celebrities. My son was one of the first people I shared the experience with. When I did, in a crushing voice, he said, "But dad I thought you were going to take me to California too." I could tell that crushed him. So I committed to making it happen, and that next summer I took him to meet his cousins, see their big house, walk Venice beach, see the Hollywood strip, hold an interview on iHeart radio, and experience Disneyland! It was definitely one of my favorite experiences as an adult, but the part he enjoyed the most was seeing his cousins— the simple things. Since then I realized that a child never forgets what's important to him or her, and will hold you to your words.

After going through financial challenges during my divorce, and as a remnant of divorce, I struggled to keep the lights on at times, and there is nothing more embarrassing to a father than having to explain that you cannot pay the light bill because of "her." Of course I never told my son about the financial strains caused by the divorce, but over time it makes you choose your promises better. So now sometimes when I answer my son's requests, I answer with a "yes" when I know it is achievable, a "no" when it is not, and a "if this happens first," so that I am not setting up his expectations to turn into disappointments.

While we're on this subject, Christ gives a sermon on making promises that we should heed and teach our children. In Matthew 5:33-37, Christ says,

> "Again you have heard that it was said to those of old, 'You shall not swear falsely, but shall perform your oaths to the Lord.' But I say to you, do not swear at all: neither by heaven, for it is God's throne; nor by the earth, for it is His footstool; nor by Jerusalem, for it is the city of the great King. Nor shall you swear by your head, because you cannot make one hair white or black. But let your 'Yes' be 'Yes,' and your 'No,' 'No.' For whatever is more than these is from the evil one."

In the early portion of that verse, Jesus is talking to the culture that says, "I promise to God..." Does that sound familiar?

Or to personalize it, "I promise I'll be at your next event, son."

Jesus is saying if you are going to do something... DO IT and do it to the glory of God. Do not set expectations that you cannot keep, nor have the power to alter.

It is always heartbreaking to hear stories from adults about empty promises that were made to their children, or the birthday gift that was "on the way in the mail," and never arrived. That impact is significant to a child, and as a parent it is unhealthy to remind your child of the empty promises the other parent made.

I will never forget about my step-dad always talking about a promise my dad made to us. He would say, "Remember when your dad promised you those footballs and basketballs, and he never got them for you?" That's likely to drive a home to become divided, and like Abraham Lincoln said, "A house divided will fall," (just playing). Jesus said it first. So too will your home if you pit your children to pick sides. Those statements penetrated for me as a kid because although my father was not active in my life he was still my father. Words like that hurt a kid, and for a long time I thought my dad did not want me, or I was "damaged goods." It impacted my confidence a great deal as a kid, and pushed me to seeking my identity more so in a gang.

However, after some maturing, the gang life appeared to be a place where all of the "damaged goods" went, and there was more fear in that lifestyle, which carried a falsehood surrounding the idea of a "true" family. Eventually, I would grow out of the gang mindset as I began to see it as more cowardly than anything. The point I am making is . . . watch the words you say and use around you children.

"

Death and life are in the power of
the tongue, And those who love it
will eat its fruit.

Proverbs 18:21 (NKJV)

"A person's heart plans his way, but the Lord determines his steps."
Proverbs 16:9 (CSB)

I would be remiss if I did not tell you to seek wise counsel at every life changing decision. Seeking wise counsel is a biblical principle we can all learn prior to establishing our plans, and it is one principle I wish I had understood sooner.

The Holy Scripture instructs us that . . .

"Plans are established by counsel; by wise counsel wage war," Proverbs 20:18 (ESV).

During my divorce, I offered to pay for the attorney fees and court fees. Since we were filing uncontested under the category of "conflict of personalities," it did not require any special type of family attorney. A co-worker had a friend he recommended, who was a practicing family attorney in a county over. Immediately, I contacted her law firm and began to obtain information regarding retainer fees and court costs. She provided me the details and submitted me a contract, with the first retainer amount of $1,300. As I was preparing my finances to pay the retainer fees, she contacted me a week later informing me that my ex-wife had obtained her own represented attorney, who was working on her case pro bono. The divorce turned from uncontested to a contested divorce, which meant the plan had to change on how things would be handled.

Once she informed me of the news, I requested that she represent me solely during the divorce. She agreed and submitted her new retainer rates, which were higher than the previous rates, and she sent over the contract for representation. As we underwent months of back and forth between attorneys regarding Discovery motions and separating household items, we could not settle on the request for child support payments. My argument was that we have joint custody and child support should not be required, because we equally have to support our son with clothing, food, daycare, shelter, medical insurance, et cetera. However, the other side pushed back harder with obtaining child support, because they felt I made more money and it would create a significantly different environment for our son. My attorney, not equipped to be an abrasive attorney, was bruised so badly with words from the other side that she would call to tell me all about how she was "yelled at."

You see I did not realize that my attorney was fairly new compared to my ex-wife's attorney, who had been practicing family law close to two decades, whereas my attorney had just recently started practicing family law about two years prior. Upon recognizing that, I felt defeated. I had already poured in close to $5,000 in court costs and lawyer fees and we were approaching one year since the paperwork was filed for the divorce with no resolve on the child support payments.

Sensing my attorney felt defeated too, she began to suggest that I pay the child support of nearly $1,500 a month. She continued to advise that the judge would likely request more if we took it to court, so to avoid being at the mercy of the judge she suggested I settle on the amount. I refused and requested to take the case before the judge. A few months later, my ex-wife and I appeared in court with our attorneys, and the judge permitted me to pay child support of about $700 and all of daycare, which was about $400 a month.

I know . . . cheap for daycare, right?

It was also less than what I was willing to settle on, but nevertheless it was a clear sign that my attorney was not operating in my best interests, so I fired her. Now, I'm broke with housing expenses, daycare, and child support. I could not afford another lawyer and began to fall behind on mortgage, utilities, and other expenses. Later, God would bless my life in a way that would allow me to rise up. As I was in the lowest point in life, God sent someone who encouraged me to keep fighting and helped me financially to hire a new attorney. Going at this the second time, I knew that my new attorney would have to have some experience. My new attorney would have to know when to argue and when to apply care to the situation. My new attorney would have to have a big heart for fathers and someone who wanted to see fathers in the lives of their children. My new attorney would not only have to possess those qualities, but would have to be as passionate about fairness as I was.

So, I searched all of the father's rights attorneys in Dallas, and found one who offered to have a free consultation with me. In a brief moment, Brandon Rasley looked me in my eyes and told me of his experience practicing family law as a father's rights attorney. He told me what he could do for me in my case since the ball was already rolling. He confidently informed me that he was not afraid of any attorney. And most importantly, he told me that he would work with me on the retainer and the finances.

Then, he honestly told me that he would not be able to completely remove child support since that was already in my temporary orders. However, he indicated that he would have it reduced to around $300 a month, and he would have the daycare split 50/50 again. Joy was restored in my heart when I heard all of what he said he could deliver on. I stood up, shook his hand and told him he was hired.

By the end of the divorce, Brandon had fulfilled all that he stated he would during our consultation. We had some tough negotiations with the other side along the way, but he was a prized contender in my corner giving me sound advice and helping me to be the father my son needed in his life.

It should be no surprise that Brandon and I are still good friends, and since then he has represented me again to completely remove child support as a whole — years after the divorce. I imagine I'll get some questions later on his contact information. Brandon was that wise counsel I needed while going through that war. He gave me options and possible results that could stem from those choices, which allowed me to make the best decisions during the divorce process. Once you have the right people in your life that can give you wise counsel, you can perform the next phase, which is establish a plan.

ESTABLISH A PLAN

Just a little over a year after the tragic events that took place on September 11, 2001, I was selected in the top 6% of the base's military personnel to travel on an all-inclusive round trip ticket for the opportunity to tour Washington D.C. What an honor, right? Well, there were a few missing details that I did not know prior to accepting this round trip ticket. For starters, it went without mention that we would have to fly there in a C-130 military cargo aircraft, which by the way only had three windows in the cargo/personnel area. Additionally, no one informed me that I would need more than a field jacket once the aircraft reached an altitude of 30,000+ feet from the ground. Nor did I know the level of noise during the flight — as the aircraft rattled above the clouds. However, the trip was the most rewarding trip an airman first class could have been assigned to take, because I experienced so much in such a short amount of time.

Aside from the uncomfortable, fishnet canopy styled seating, I did have a wonderful experience. Although I was fairly new to the Air Force base, located in the country woods of Jacksonville, Arkansas, I had a specialty that allowed me to meet face-to-face with the group commanders assigned to the base. I had actually built a rapport with many of them especially the Operations Group Commander, who happened to be the co-pilot during our flight.

While in-flight at 30,000+ feet, I was invited to see the trip from the cockpit of the aircraft, which I had never experienced until then! Talk about a breathtaking experience and it was definitely better than sitting in the canopy seating. When we arrived at Andrews Air Force Base, we deplaned and were transported to a fancy four-star hotel not too far from Georgetown.

Since I had heard so much about Washington D.C., and with it being our nation's capitol, I was excited to see what it had to offer. That night, despite the time difference and serious jetlag I would experience the next couple of mornings, I went walking down the dark streets of D.C. and found myself with a group of equally excited airmen looking to experience the nightlife of the nation's capital as well. Keep in mind this was before social media, GPS on our cell phones, or Yelp. In fact, cell phones had pretty basic functions. We could call and text AND that was about it. We relied heavily on actual paper maps to get around, such as road atlases. Don't worry there will not be a quiz over the technology of my day at the end of this book. However, we have come a mighty long way since then! Walking the streets of D.C., without any real plans of where to go, we found ourselves on the Metro, which was another first-time experience for me as a native Texan. I recall thinking "it couldn't be as complicated as catching a bus, right?" Wrong. It was so confusing trying to determine where the blue line and the green line went that we had to stop and ask a local resident how we could get back to our hotel. Eventually, we would figure out the train system, but that first night was one adventure that seemed scary at moments as we navigated in unfamiliar territory. However, by God's grace, He navigated us safely back to the comfort of our cozy suite. Around 0630, the next morning, we woke up to have breakfast and depart for the first journey of our tour, the battlefield of Manassas/Bull Run.

The weather was freezing cold around 30°F. Yet there was morning dew and fog seemed to cover the land where the canons once fired. I recall thinking how eerie and authentic the scene looked, as we stood on the grounds where many soldiers had lost their lives over a hundred years before us. We walked the battlefield in deep somber thought. Realizing that we would have to go to war one day, and death on the battlefield could be our fate as well. I could feel the passion of both sides; as if the spirits of those soldiers were still fighting a war they felt passionately about.

Manassas (Bull Run) was the first major land battle of the American Civil War, where 35,000 Union troops, lead by Brigadier General Irvin McDowell, marched from Washington D.C. to seize a Confederate headquarters in Manassas Junction, Virginia. This assault was in response to an attack made at Fort Sumter by Confederate soldiers. President Lincoln gave the orders to mount an offense, and although the general requested more time to train the troops, the President insisted that the Confederate soldiers were equally amateurs in the arts of war.

Following orders, the general and his troops marched forward. When the troops arrived at Manassas they were greeted with what may have seemed like a measly 20,000 Confederate soldiers. However, as history would record it, the Confederate troops were able to break the Union's right flank and began to rush Union soldiers, causing the Union's army to retreat back to Washington D.C. This critical battle gave Confederates a boost of confidence throughout the South, while the North came to a realization that it was not going to be an easy conflict as they had suspected. Thinking back on this battle, clearly the Union had more manpower than the Confederates, so it seemed like an easy victory. I'm sure that's exactly what President Lincoln thought going into battle; however, as Lincoln would discover later during the American Civil War, a readiness level was required and leaders were also needed to lead courageously.

You may be asking, "What does any of this have to do with co-parenting or raising my child in a single parent home?" I'm so glad you asked. Because if you really examined those two experiences you will see discomfort and fear all because of poor planning. You will see assumptions being made, which in the case of the Union soldiers, during the battle at Manassas, resulted in defeat. Moreover, as it pertains to Manassas, you will see no real executable plan leading to a successful outcome—well depending on which side you're on.

When developing your parenting plan you want to focus on being clear and as detailed as possible, while keeping in mind that your child will not stay the same age forever. I know that's a challenge in itself because we want them to stay the same age, but reality is reality. Also, realize that you will not think of every possible situation or encounter your child will go through in life. Your co-parenting plan should be a living-breathing document that allows for flexibility as needed, and can grow over time.

THE DEVIL IN THE DETAILS

The expression, "the devil is in the details," has been used for years and usually suggests that a person carefully examine the small print of a document or contract prior to accepting its terms. The "details" in your family plan should equally be examined to the point that there is no room for assumptions or doubts when it comes to your child *between homes*. Although, there is nothing legally binding about a co-parenting plan it serves as your agreed upon terms with raising your child. It holds each parent accountable to standing on his or her word. At the back of the book, you will find resources to help you get started on creating your own custom co-parenting plan. Also, if you are a single parent and there is no partnership with the other parent currently, it would still serve you well to develop a parenting plan for yourself. This will help you as a guide to remain consistent as you hold yourself accountable to how you will reward, discipline, establish your child's bedtime, and/or introduce them to a significant other in your life. Establishing sound and detailed plans are necessary as your child grows and develops.

Parenting plans offer consistency and create routines in your child's life. Routines and consistency are important to a child and helps them in developing a sense of security. As a matter of fact, children tend to thrive in environments around caregivers that provide them with dependable and close relationships. Furthermore, in these early stages of development, if there is not at least one close relationship, the child's development can become disrupted and can have permanent and lasting effects. As we discussed in the chapter entitled, "Matters of the Heart," your health and wellbeing as a parent matter to the early development stages of your child. This is not something you should take lightly.

Early during my separation, actually a couple weeks before the separation had begun, my son's mother and I worked out a plan. Neither one of us really wanted to give up our role in the life of our son, so after a tough cry over the reality of it all, we began to create a plan that would allow us to both have an active role in our son's life. We started by understanding how important both of us were to our son, and how each of us has a unique and special purpose in his life. The last thing I wanted to do was rip our son from his mother, and his mother felt the same toward me.

There were also routines my son and I had developed and as a committed father, I refused to break them. Every night just before bed, my son would bring me one of his favorite books that he would want me to read to him. My most memorable moments were when his eyes would light up when I would change my voice to the different characters in the stories. It made story time exciting for him each night. After reading one to two books, depending on how much time until bedtime, we would say prayers together on the side of his bed. These were memories I often had as a kid praying with my grandmother on the side of her bed, and it felt rewarding to share those values with my son. Once we would finish praying, I would tuck him into bed and I would sing two songs: "Jesus Loves You" and "I Love You." When the last song was sung I would kiss him, tell him that I loved him, and wished him good night. Now those are moments you cannot get back!

That Sunday evening, his mother and I had created our very first co-parenting agreement by setting our custody exchange terms between each other. We agreed to alternate weeks starting our custody exchange days on Thursdays, which later modified to Fridays, and we arranged the pick up and drop off to daycare in a way that allowed us both to see our son throughout the month (minus four days each). As our son grew, and as his mother and I battled on through a two-year divorce, one thing that rarely changed was our initial parenting plan and child custody exchange agreement.

Since typing out anything that looked formal on paper was a bit frightening, considering the divorce climate and going back and forth between attorneys, much of what we would agree on occurred through text messaging and emails. This is okay too, as long as you find a way to retain the messages or transcribe them into a word document documenting the agreement for your safekeeping and clarity. Because we all know how fragile smartphones can be when we drop them it is probably better to almost immediately transcribe the information or find ways to retain it until you are able to transcribe to a document. For my son's mother and I, these early communications were cornerstones in the foundation of what was to come in our final divorce decree and for our future along the path of partnership.

I want to talk to the guys for just a second. It becomes so easy to throw your hands up and put the fate of your parenting and child custody plan in the hands of the judge, and I will be the first to say there is a time and a place to surrender to the mercy of the judge, and there are times when you need to lay a foundation before it reaches the judge. Don't get me wrong, a judge will make the decision for you and usually there is a "one size fits all" custody agreement they have prepared and have no problem enforcing. Taken from my experience, having a plan helped as a guiding light as we began to work through discipline and the transfer of custody. Additionally, a plan showed the judge that I was not going to be the "status quo" type of father. The reality is that many men are not the "status quo" type, however, we have been grouped with many others who are the exact definition of status quo. How do we get ahead of that? It's simple . . . we live above the status quo standards. One way to live above the status quo standards is to set our standard on a higher level by measuring our lives according to the Bible. As fathers, that means we have to be active in our child's life and by becoming the biblical example of a father who lives like Christ. Creating a formal plan helps us to remember what we said we would do as a father. It is highly recommended to establish a parenting plan before emotions get too high. Once a person's emotions are high we can become highly irrational in our negotiations.

Now that we have that out of the way, let's talk about the x-factor. Everyone who reads this book will not have the same parenting plan. We all live busy, crazy, and sometimes hectic lives that require our parenting plan to be modified from time to time, or just works better one way over the other. For instance, I spoke about my custody exchange days being on Fridays. Based on our work schedules, at that time, and us working on opposite ends of the city, that day worked best for us. It also gave each parent a full weekend off to just relax, go out with friends, or spend time doing other activities. Your days may be on Wednesdays. The most important thing is that you have a plan.

"

A person's heart plans his way, but the Lord determines his steps.

Proverbs 16:9 (CSB)

"Every good and perfect gift is from above, coming down from the Father of lights, who does not change like shifting shadows."
James 1:17 (CSB)

On June 21, 2018, I made the biggest decision of my life: to get married . . . again. Yes, that's right for a second time! This time understanding what it means to be equally yoked. That Thursday seemed like the shortest day in history as I prepared for the events that would take place later that evening. The irony is it was actually the longest day because I had planned a wedding proposal on the day of summer solstice, which happens to be the longest day of the year.

I had planned a nice evening away from it all and took my soon-to-be fiancé, Tanasha, out to dinner at a place on the edge of downtown Dallas, called Stampede 66. The evening was perfect and we did not have to battle with the crowds, nor did we have to wait in line. As we sat down to look at the menu, the manager came over with complimentary deviled eggs. At $12, that was a significant gesture especially with it being our first time visiting. It left a lasting impression on us both. As we continued to decide on our entree, we "ran into a mutual friend." This mutual friend happened to be my accomplice in staging the biggest proposal in my history and he was there to film it. Acting like he was filming a video for the restaurant, he came over with the manager, and pretended to discuss the project, which is when my fiancé noticed him. "We know him!" She yelled at the waitress. As our friend turned to acknowledge her response, we "caught up" briefly over the project he was filming "for the restaurant." Once he left the table, after indicating he would return to get footage of our food, both of us left for the restroom to wash up and to prepare for our meal. Little did my sweet love know, I was getting my microphone clipped on and was plotting an epic evening. Upon returning to the table I made up a story, since she saw both of us coming out of the restroom. I told her that I had a brief conversation about how he found this job. She proceeded to ask me how, and I told her it was a referral.

Then, our friend appeared at our table to get some quick footage and he referred to the video project, which aligned perfectly (even though the stories were not planned or rehearsed). Once we ate our meals we continued on to the next surprise. Before we left, we gave a quick testimonial video about our date and the delicious meal we enjoyed. After our testimonial, we proceeded on to the Reunion Tower (my fiancé was blindfolded the whole trip). After a bunch of walking, one tricky escalator ride, and an elevator ride that exposed the location. Finally, we arrived on the GeO-Deck platform of the Reunion Tower, which is where I proposed to my better half. She said "YES" of course and she was completely surprised.

She shared the news with her son, whom I had built a close relationship with over the course of she and I dating. Just over two weeks prior to the proposal, I asked her son, Jacob, for his blessing to take his mother's hand. He gave me his blessing. After hearing the news, he could not wait to call his mother. We filled him in on the details later that night, and it was such a blessing to see his face light up with joy. Another joyful moment took place the next day as we headed to Six Flags of Texas as a soon-to-be blended family, and my son, Christian said, "This is the best day of my life, because I already have two dads, and now I am going to have two moms and two brothers *(his mother and stepdad had a baby boy just a year ago)*!"

That was such a revealing testimony of how God takes your pain, struggles, hardships, and challenges then turns it into something that brings Him glory and brings you joy. I once feared being married again. It seemed like the odds were stacked against those who gave "love" a second, or even a third chance. Statistics have given re-marriages an even higher divorce percentage at 60-67% on a second marriage, and 73-74% on a third marriage. I can only imagine what the statistics of divorce would be on a fourth marriage.

My grandmother was the anomaly and experienced 22 years of marriage until my grandfather passed away. Clearly, she did not give up on love like many would have done after the first divorce, and neither did I. And I suppose, when you know love is Yahweh, it is very hard to give up on someone who has not given up on you.

I think about the story of Job when I go through challenges. Often, I am thinking of it from the perspective of having everything and losing it, never to regain it again. However there is a restoration process that takes place with Job. We see in Job 42:10 that he was restored twice the wealth, family, and possessions he had before. God is a restorer. He is a healer, and most importantly He is the Source that has promised those who love Him a future.

Jeremiah 29:11 was a reminder to me that God has a plan for my life and it is a plan to prosper, to give me hope, and to have a future. Sometimes I think we forget that. When we get in our valleys as parents, we tend to be consumed with anxiety and fear. The good news for us, as children of God, is we know who to give that anxiety to, and we know who can chase out fear . . . God! Jesus says in Matthew 11:28–30 (CSB):

"Come to me, all of you who are weary and burdened, and I will give you rest. Take up my yoke and learn from me, because I am lowly and humble in heart, and you will find rest for your souls. For my yoke is easy and my burden is light."

That gives me comfort—to know that someone has chosen to lift the burden from my shoulders. All I have to do is take up His yoke and learn His ways of being lowly and humble in heart. In the KSV, Jesus is saying, "If you learn these things from Me you can be carefree too." Life would be so much easier if everyone was carefree. However, that is not the world we live in, is it? In fact, a study reported by the Huffington Post, showed that 85% of what subjects worried about did not actually happen, and they showed that 97% of what a person worries about is fear driven by exaggerations and misconceptions. Fear can become a distraction from being the parent you are called to be, and it will lead you to acting irrational, considering that it is an emotion. Fear is also an emotional survival mechanism we use to propel our strength or it can cause us to plan evil or spiteful actions. The Word of God says there is no fear in perfect love. 1 John 4:18 (CSB) says,

> "There is no fear in love; instead, perfect love drives out fear, because fear involves punishment. So the one who fears is not complete in love."

I alluded to this earlier in the book; however, I want to take the time to really drive home the message that God does not want you to be defeated. He does not want you to be a passive parent. He does WANT you to become complete in love, so that you no longer have fear of what could or would happen.

Live boldly in love, truth, and understanding. No matter the difficulty, no matter the struggle, no matter the challenge. Know confidently, without a doubt, that you will persevere as a co-parent or single parent. You have a purpose as a parent, which the Bible has provided. Draw closer to God and develop an intimate relationship with Him. He wants to be your Source—who you find strength and courage through. Allow God to direct your steps as you seek wise counsel and establish a parenting plan that will hold you accountable to your responsibilities as a parent, and if you are co-parenting, it will hold you both to your responsibilities.

My hope is that this book has planted a seed or has watered a seed that has been growing within, and it is my desire that the words in this book have allowed you to understand why it is so important to focus on the child *Between Homes*. Before we close this chapter, however, I think it is only right to close it in prayer. As we pray, I want you to think of the challenges that you have currently on your heart. I want you to also think about what areas of your life you would like to see increase, and most importantly what desires you have for your children. Let's pray . . .

Holy God, our Father, our Protector, our Defender, our Truth, and our Love. We come in reverence of Your glory that is magnified through all things and around all things. You are Mighty and just. We ask for forgiveness of our failed attempts to live right. We ask for a heart that forgives others of their offenses toward us. Your Light shines through us, and through that light we ask for joy, peace, and increase in the areas of our lives that we have placed on our hearts. We know that there is power in You and the glorious name of Christ Jesus. We lift You up as our True Redeemer . . . our Fortress . . . and our SHIELD! Change our challenges into courage, and our burdens into blessings. We ask it all in the name of Jesus Christ, Amen.

"

Every good and perfect gift is from above, coming down from the Father of lights, who does not change like shifting shadows.

James 1:17 (CSB)

Letter to the Reader

Dear Reader,

Hopefully, this book was encouraging, and inspired you in ways to live better and to depend on God while raising your child in a single or co-parent home.

If this book has impacted your life in any way, please feel free to send me an email at **contact@kennethactsout.com**, and tell me about it.

I look forward to the blessings that God has stored for you and your family to receive. May God bless you and keep you always.

Godspeed,

Kenneth Spresley

Helpful Resources

Study Bible Resources

- ☐ BlueLetterBible.org

- ☐ BibleStudyTools.com

- ☐ CCEL.org

- ☐ GotQuestions.org

Parenting Resources

- ☐ www.mayoclinic.org/healthy-lifestyle/childrens-health/in-depth/single-parent/art-20046774

- ☐ singleparentadvocate.org

- ☐ childreninthemiddle.com/

Example of Co-Parenting Plan

This parenting plan is between (Parent 1), the father, and (Parent 2), the mother, and details how each parent will raise, discipline, reward, and bring up (Child/ren). This agreement can be altered at any time by mutual agreement, and should be used as a living document, which is adjusted based on the needs of the parents and the child/ren.

The father and the mother mutually agree as follows:

> The best interests of the minor child/ren will be maintained through appropriate involvement of both mother and father in each child's life.
> Both parents agree that each parent is a fit and proper person to be involved in the parenting of the child/children.
>
> Both parents will remain active and appropriately involved in maintaining a safe, stable consistent and nurturing relationship with their child/children.
>
> The overriding purpose of this plan will be to establish custody, parenting time, visitation and other access arrangements to include apportionment of parenting time to be spent with both parents and to provide provisions for a remediation process regarding future modifications of this plan, if needed.
>
> Both parents understand the needs of each child/children may change as the child/children develop and they will interpret and apply this plan in a way which best serves the evolving interests of each child/children.
>
> The parties understand that this Plan anticipates they will act in the best interest of each minor child/children as defined by state law.

Both parents shall have joint legal custody of the child/children which requires that they exercise mutual authority and responsibility for making final fundamental regarding each child/children's welfare and mutually participate in the responsibility of providing the parenting functions necessary for raising child/children.

One parent may not plan or schedule activities for a child/children during the parenting time of the other parent, without reasonable notice and consent of the other parent.

Both parents shall inform one another reasonably in advance of each child/children's events where a parent may participate in the child/children's activities or events (for example, school plays, teacher conferences, sporting events, music recitals, et cetera). Notice shall be provided in such a way that the other parent has the maximum opportunity to attend that activity or event.

Both parents will maintain an appropriate bedtime for the child/ren of _____ p.m.

Both parents also agree that discipline should be executed only by and between each parent, and should be reasonable based on the age, offense, and mental capabilities of understanding.

ACKNOWLEDGMENT OF PARENTING PLAN

By signing this Parenting Plan, we approve the terms and conditions of our agreement. We believe the Parenting Plan as set forth above is in the best interests of each of our children. We each have agreed to this

Parenting Plan with full understanding and without undue influence, fraud, coercion, or misrepresentation. Our full agreement is set forth herein, and there are no secret or undisclosed terms. We agree to abide by the general principles set forth herein.

_____   _____
Father's Signature   **Date**

_____   _____
Mother's Signature   **Date**

Notes

1. http://www.pewresearch.org/fact-tank/2014/12/22/less-than-half-of-u-s-kids-today-live-in-a-traditional-family/
2. Myers, D. "Psychology (Eighth Edition)."
3. http://www.history.org/almanack/life/family/black.cfm
4. https://www.mountvernon.org/library/digitalhistory/digital-encyclopedia/article/slavery-and-marriage/
5. http://www.chicagotribune.com/news/columnists/glanton/ct-opioid-epidemic-dahleen-glanton-met-20170815-column.html
6. https://www.bjs.gov/content/pub/pdf/jim14.pdf
7. https://www.law.cornell.edu/constitution/constitution.amendmentxiii.html
8. https://www.gotquestions.org/mothers-Christian.html
9. https://www.gotquestions.org/fathers-Christian.html
10. https://www.youtube.com/watch?v=u82j8FYy7OM
11. https://www.history.com/topics/american-civil-war/first-battle-of-bull-run
12. http://www.divorcestatistics.info/divorce-statistics-and-divorce-rate-in-the-usa.html
13. https://www.huffingtonpost.com/don-joseph-goewey-/85-of-what-we-worry-about_b_8028368.html

Scripture Index